What is Wisdom?
(And where do I find it?)

By Jack Pransky
and Amy Kahofer

Illustrations
T.M. Du...

What is Wisdom (and Where Do I Find It)?
Jack Pransky and Amy Kahofer
Illustrations by T. M. DuSablon

© 2016 Jack Pransky and Amy Kahofer

All rights reserved. This book may not be copied in its entirety for any reason.

ISBN: 978-1-517513-8-32
Publisher Information: 3 Principles Publications
www.insideoutunderstanding.com

This book was printed and bound in South Carolina by Createspace.
This book may be ordered online at www.amazon.com or www.insideoutunderstanding.com.

For information and questions regarding this book please email via www.insideoutunderstanding.com.

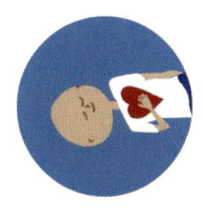

Reader Praise for
What is Wisdom? (And where do I find it?)

After two pages I found myself reading this book aloud to an invisible group of children gathered at my feet! I was hooked and knew immediately that young children would be too. *What is Wisdom* is a perfect springboard for the important conversations we need to have - a delightful segue to helping children uncover their own wisdom. I LOVED it.

--Barb Aust, BEd, MEd, retired Principal
Author, *The Essential Curriculum*

Children, clients and grown-ups of all ages will resonate with the advice of owl and tortoise: a gentle reminder to slow down, ignore the chatter in the head and listen to the heart. Thank you, Jack and Amy, for making this life-changing message so easy to hear and share.

--Nancy Lopin, M.A., 3 Principles group facilitator,
Suffolk County House of Correction, Boston, MA

Jack and Amy have found a simple, yet beautiful, way to teach young children how to access the wisdom that is always available to them in a quiet mind. This is such a valuable lesson that I hope it will become available to every elementary school.

--Lori Carpenos, LMFT
author, *It's an Inside-Out World*

Wisdom is such an important topic. Jack Pransky and Amy Kahofer have written this for younger kids, but having worked with learners from K-12 I know all learners love picture books and I know all learners would love this book. At school or at home, read and discuss this wonderful story to get a glimpse inside! Bravo! Great book.

--Christa Campsall, B.Ed., Dipl.Sp.Ed., M.A.
and 3 Principles Ed Talks at (ed-talks.com)

What a wonderful book to be able to share with children. It points us towards where wisdom hides, for all of us, inside ourselves. As Jack and Amy say, wisdom is behind all the noise, slow down, quieten the mind and it's there! I would thoroughly recommend this book for any child from three years to ninety. Like all excellent books it is, in equal measures, thought provoking touching and fun. It speaks to that special part in all of us... It is a great little book that I can't wait to share with the children I work with.

-- Peter Anderson Cert, Edn. Adv. Dip.(Cambs).
Headteacher of five schools for over thirty years

I have used Jack and Amy's previous children's book *What Is a Thought? (A Thought Is a Lot)* for lunch clubs in an elementary school in London and at after school clubs for children in Israel. I found that through the lesson plans, story and illustrations, the children not only gained an immense amount by having a newfound confidence in all areas, they also really enjoyed it and it was great fun! As a teacher, it was so helpful for me to have an immediately available lesson plan. I am very excited for *What is Wisdom (and Where Do I Find it)?* to get out to people. Having read through it I am confident that this will have the same impact as 'What is a Thought'. In my mind, what greater gift can you give a child then helping him or her access their own wisdom?

-Shifra Chesler (Rosenblatt), Innate Health practitioner,
New Thought Consultancy. Jerusalem, Isreal

GREAT book, which I would definitely recommend for any child/class whether they are experiencing bullying or any other issues great or small... and who doesn't? I honestly love it!!! The questions are also a big help, as this book should be read more than once and taken apart during subsequent readings for better understanding.

--Celeste Gonzalez, Early Childhood and Elementary Education Teacher with the New York City school system, Bronx, New York

What is Wisdom? is simply delightful. Jack Pransky and Amy Kahofer share an essential message that all children must hear. This book is an invitation to parents and educators to engage in conversation with young people about the importance of seeing their internal treasure. This story will surely catch the curiosity of both children and adults about this most beautiful gift for humanity. it's a wonderful book. Can't wait to share it with others.

--Quinn Cashion, MEdL, Education Consultant, British Columbia
Author, *Building Resilience from the Inside-Out Training Manual*

❊

Reader Praise for
What is A Thought? (A Thought is a Lot)

This gorgeously illustrated story is exactly what every early childhood educator and clinician needs - a way to explain the unexplainable: thoughts lead to feelings! The original artwork and winning rhyme are perfect for engaging children in reflective discussions on the abstract concept of a thought. An outstanding book with stimulating lesson plans that my staff and I will use with all our clients with language, learning, and social cognitive challenges.

--Nancy Tarshis MA, MS CCC-SLP
Supervisor of Speech and Languages Services at the Children's Evaluation and Rehabilitation Center at Einstein College of Medicine

I absolutely loved your book *What is a Thought? (A thought is a Lot)*! I loved the simplicity and yet the power that lies underneath the words. When I heard the book read on the radio, I was moved. It is an amazing book written for kids, but one adults could benefit from tremendously for themselves.

--Sunil "Sunny" Punjabi, Teacher, Hong Kong

Dedication

To all the teachers in the world who work with children, and to all the parents who raise them.

And to Eden Rose.
May you always be guided by wisdom.

Acknowledgements

To Syd Banks, for his inspiration.
And to Nancy Lopin, for her editorial assistance.

Introduction

What is Wisdom (and Where Do I Find It)? is a sequel to *What is a Thought? (A Thought is a Lot!)* by Jack Pransky and Amy Kahofer, following the same little guy into deeper exploration within. It also serves as a stand-alone book.

What is Wisdom... introduces children to the amazing power within us all called wisdom. Its purpose is to help children and adults alike, through an engaging, well-illustrated story, to realize where wisdom comes from, how we can access it when needed, how it can keep us out of trouble and how it can guide us well through life.

The authors have witnessed the amazing power this idea holds, both for our own lives and for the lives of people with whom we have worked. We believe sharing this important message from an early age can lead to healthier choices and behaviors at any age.

What is Wisdom (and Where Do I Find It)?, like *What is a Thought? (A Thought is a Lot!)* before it, gives children new hope that they can rise above whatever the situations or circumstances in which they feel stuck. It teaches that wisdom arises from deep inside oneself and is always available to us when our mind clears or when our typical thinking calms or subsides. Wisdom is truly an awesome gift! Wonderful original artwork enhances this simple, yet profound, message. Older children can read this book on their own; younger children can have an adult read it to them. A set of questions to aid understanding of this sometimes abstract notion is provided for teachers and parents, along with an "Art Glossary." The authors also point to the lesson plans with experiential activities and handouts depicted in *What is a Thought...* that pertain specifically to the wisdom story of this book, all of which will help in a child-friendly way teach the sometimes abstract notion of wisdom.

We all have the power to allow wisdom to guide us in whatever situation we encounter. It can be used to our benefit. It starts with knowing what wisdom really is, and where we can find it.

What is wisdom?
Will it come when I'm old?
Where do I find it?
How will I know?

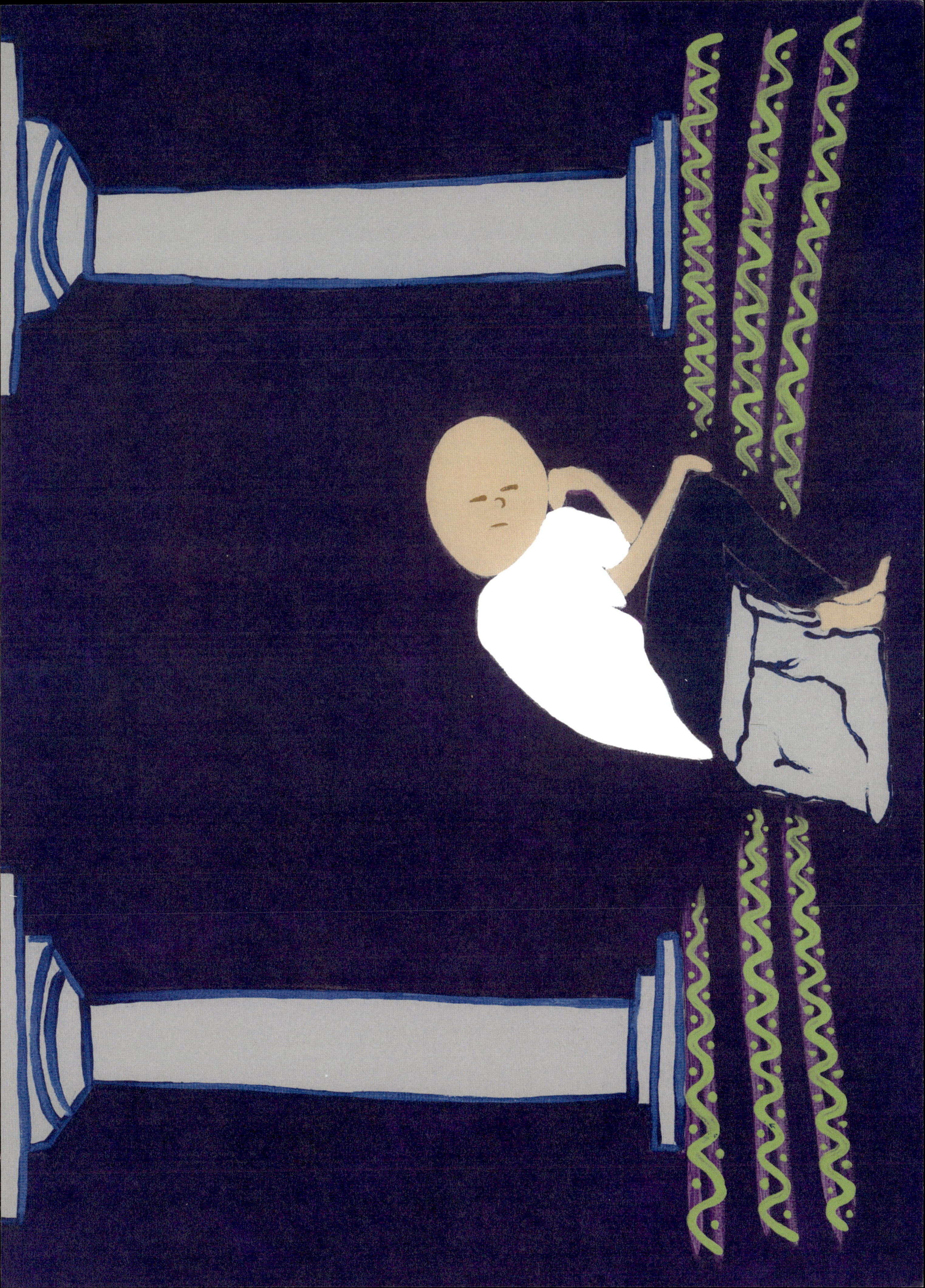

Wisdom is a big word,
A word that sounds so wise,
That seems to come from
A person twice my size.

What does wisdom look like?
What will it do for me?

Maybe a story will help us see...

WISDOM

Once upon a time
There was a little guy
Who wanted so bad to find wisdom
He just had to try.

He looked in his drawers.
He looked up the stairs.
He looked under the covers.
He looked under the chairs.

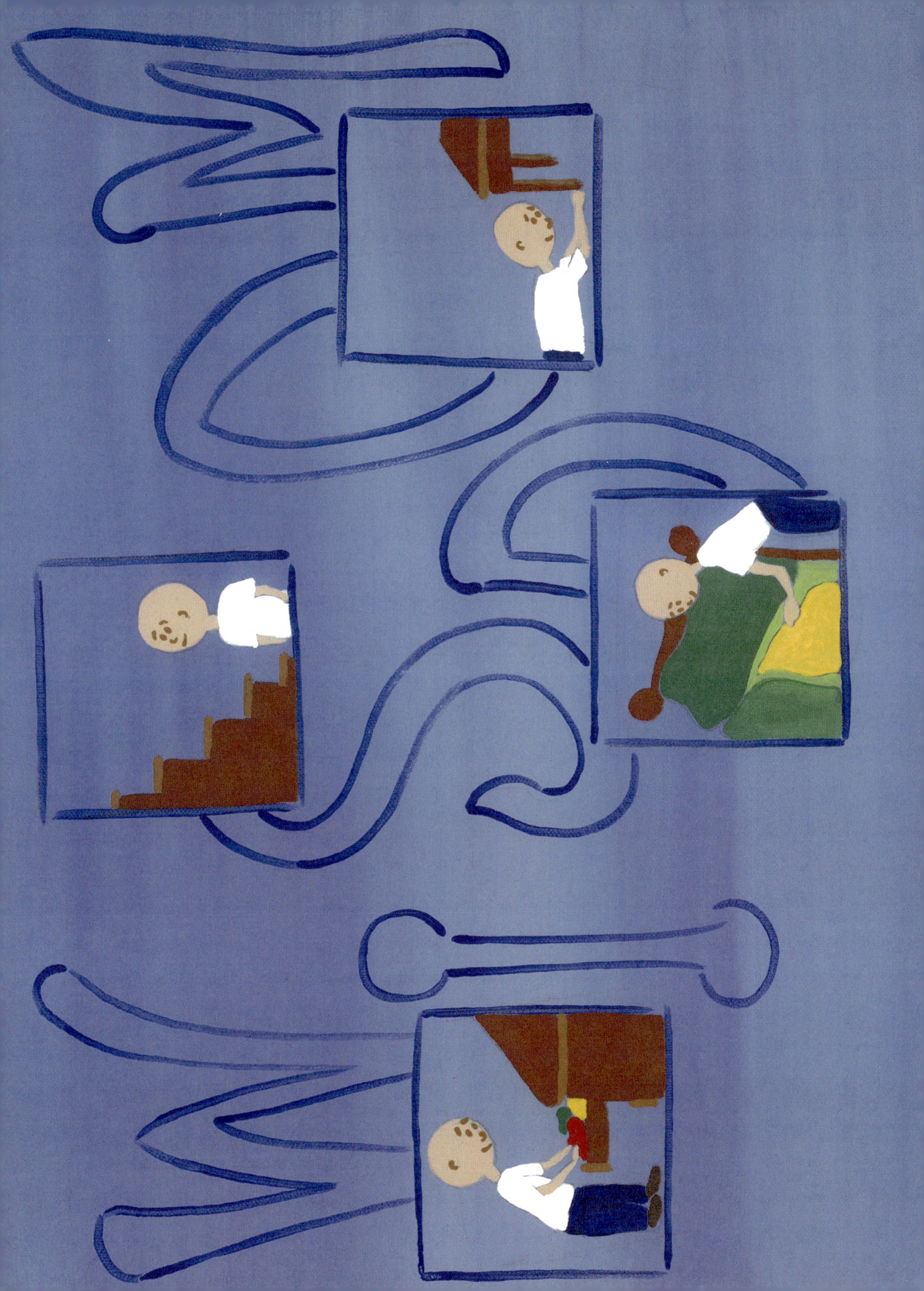

He climbed to the tree tops
And went out on a limb.
He searched in the grass.
But it didn't find him.

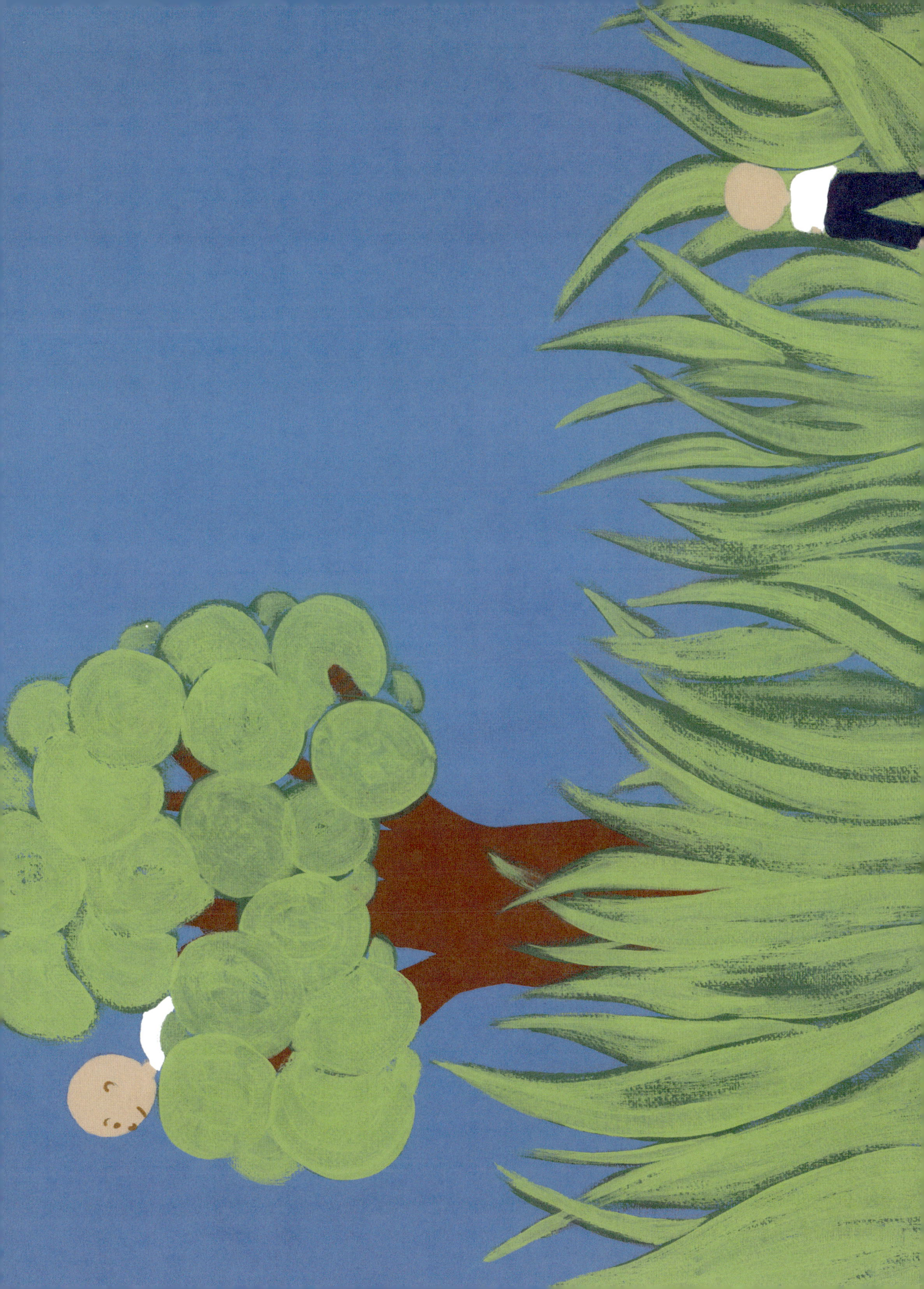

So he went and asked the owl
Whoooo was supposed to be so wise.
But the owl only shrugged his shoulders
And let out a big sigh.

"I don't know how I know,"
Was all the owl said.
"I just get a feeling.
It's not in my head."

"Huh?" said little guy,
"That doesn't help me.
"I don't understand…"
"But, wait… maybe…"

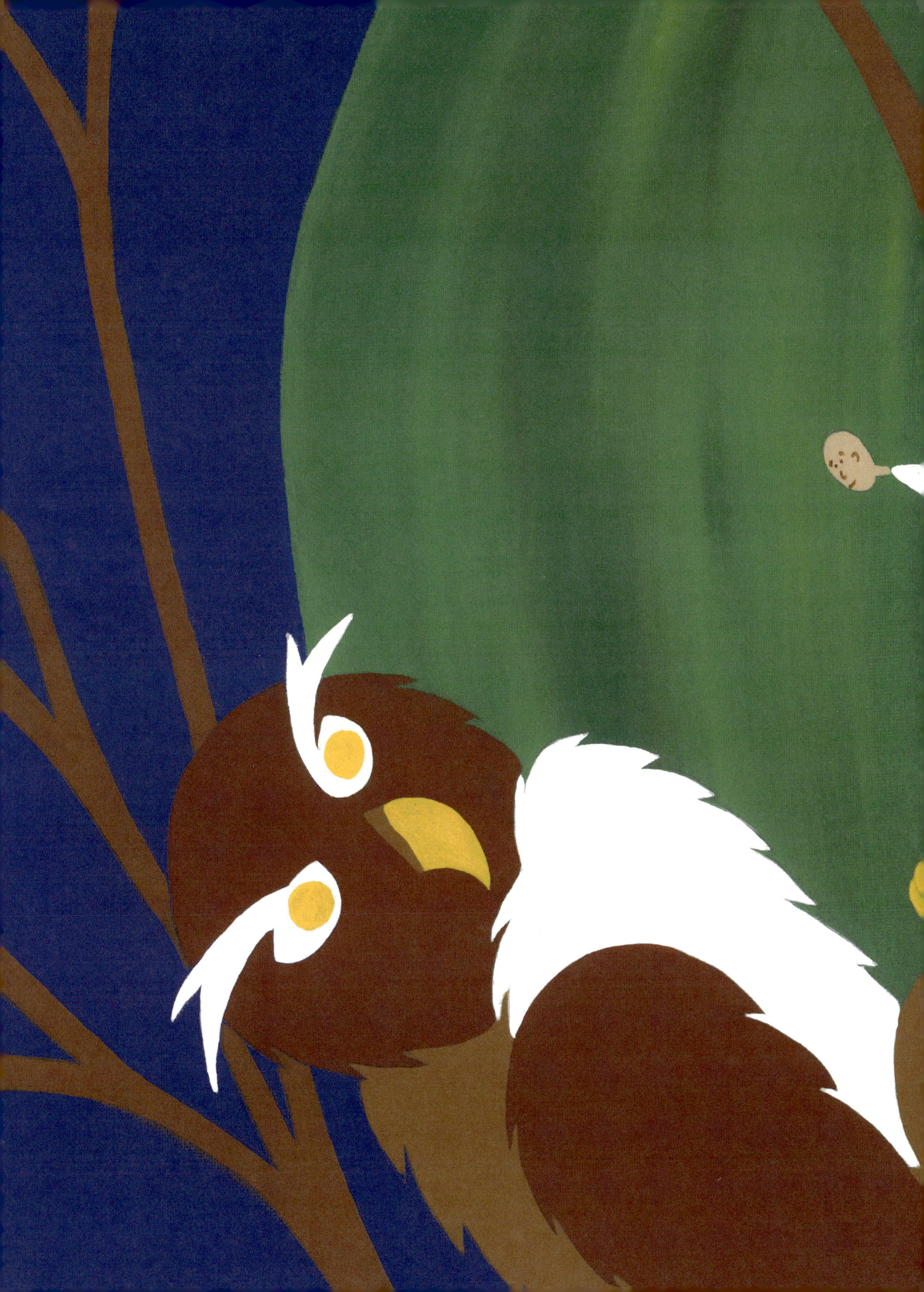

Maybe we can't get wisdom from anything out there
Or from what we make up in our head.
Maybe it's something that can only come
From within our heart instead.

But if it's something inside me
And I've had it all along,
Why can't I always find it?
It doesn't always feel so strong.

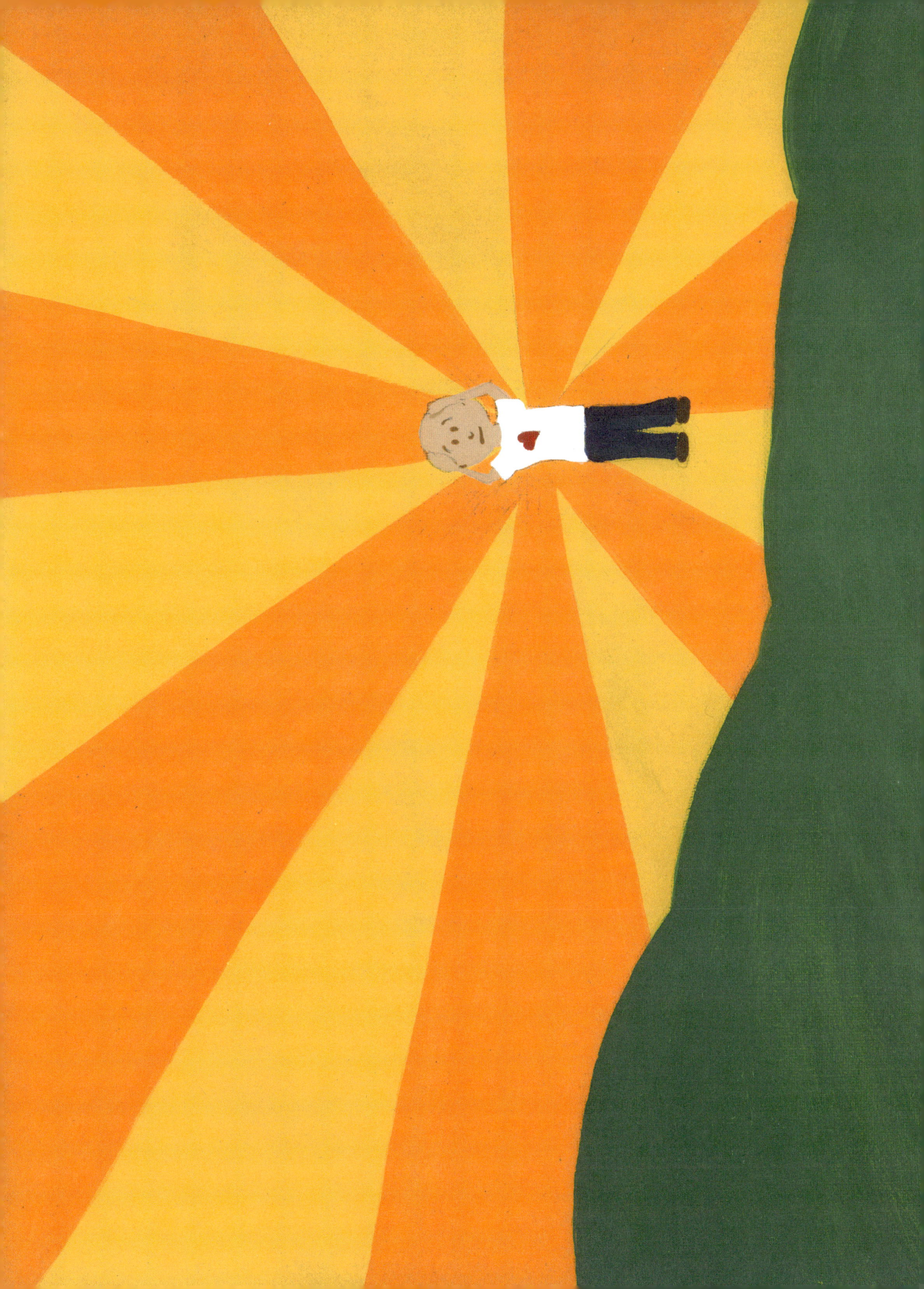

So he went to ask Old Tortoise,
Knocked on his door.
Old Tortoise just said, "Son, slow down."
He said not one thing more.

"What do you mean, 'Slow down?'
Was that all you said?"
Old Tortoise whispered, "That's the secret."
Then he tucked in his head.

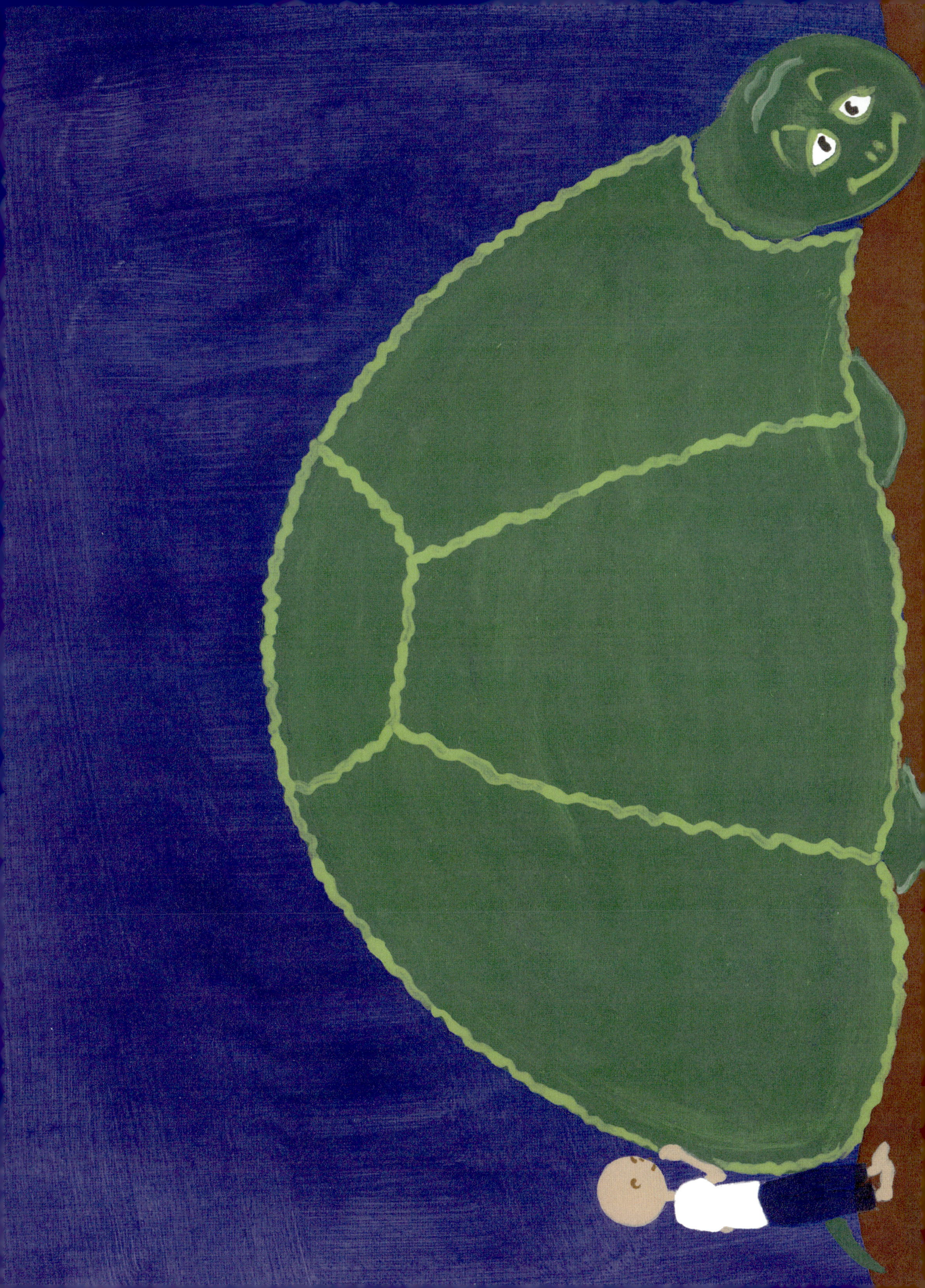

Little guy became even more confused.
"I give up!" he cried.
And that's exactly when the answer
Popped into his mind.

"Ah ha! Now I know!"
He jumped with joy.
"I get it!
Wisdom is behind all the noise!"

All day long my thoughts talk loud
And race inside my head.
Only when my mind slows down can I hear it.
But my thoughts run too fast instead.

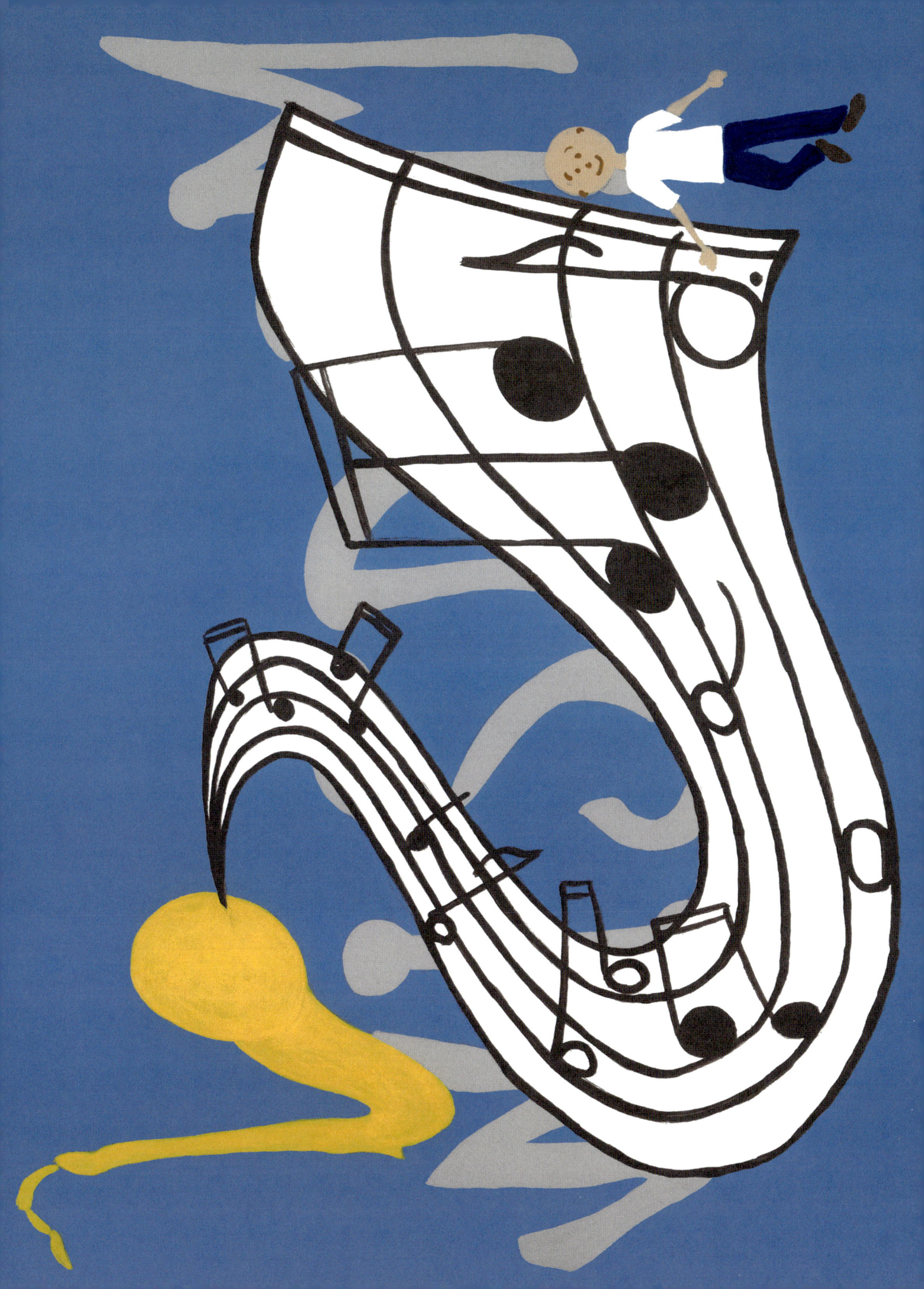

If I just give myself time to let my mind calm down
And let my thoughts pass by,
The wisdom inside will just pop up
And I won't even have to try.

Wow, that means wisdom
is who I really am!
If I don't know the answer,
When my mind clears, I can!

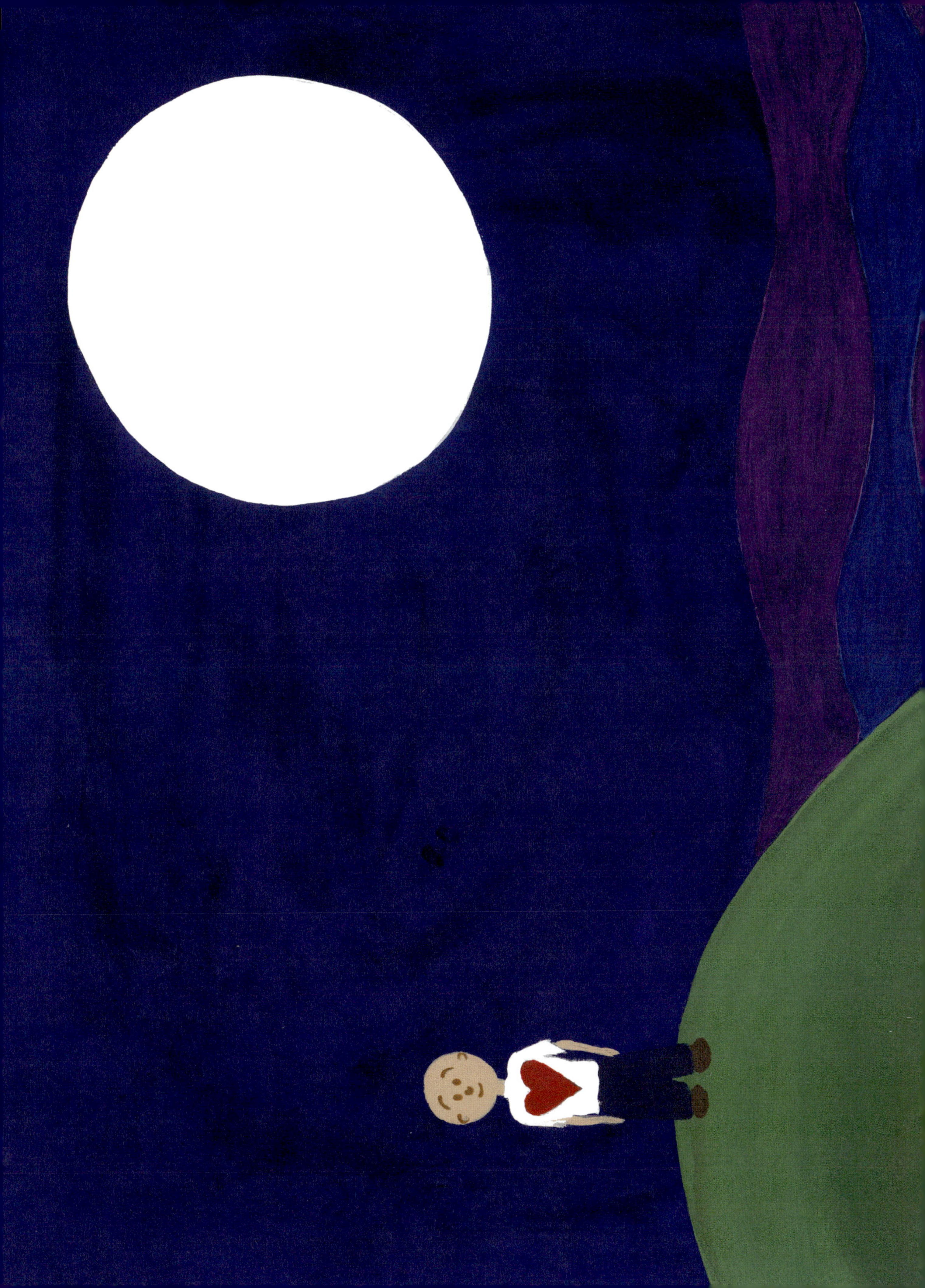

So now when I'm mad
Or sit alone and cry,
I'll know that wisdom
Is always right nearby.

I'll never be alone again
Because I've got wisdom as my friend.

But we have to be quiet
And listen real close,
Because anger or hurt
Can talk loudest and most.

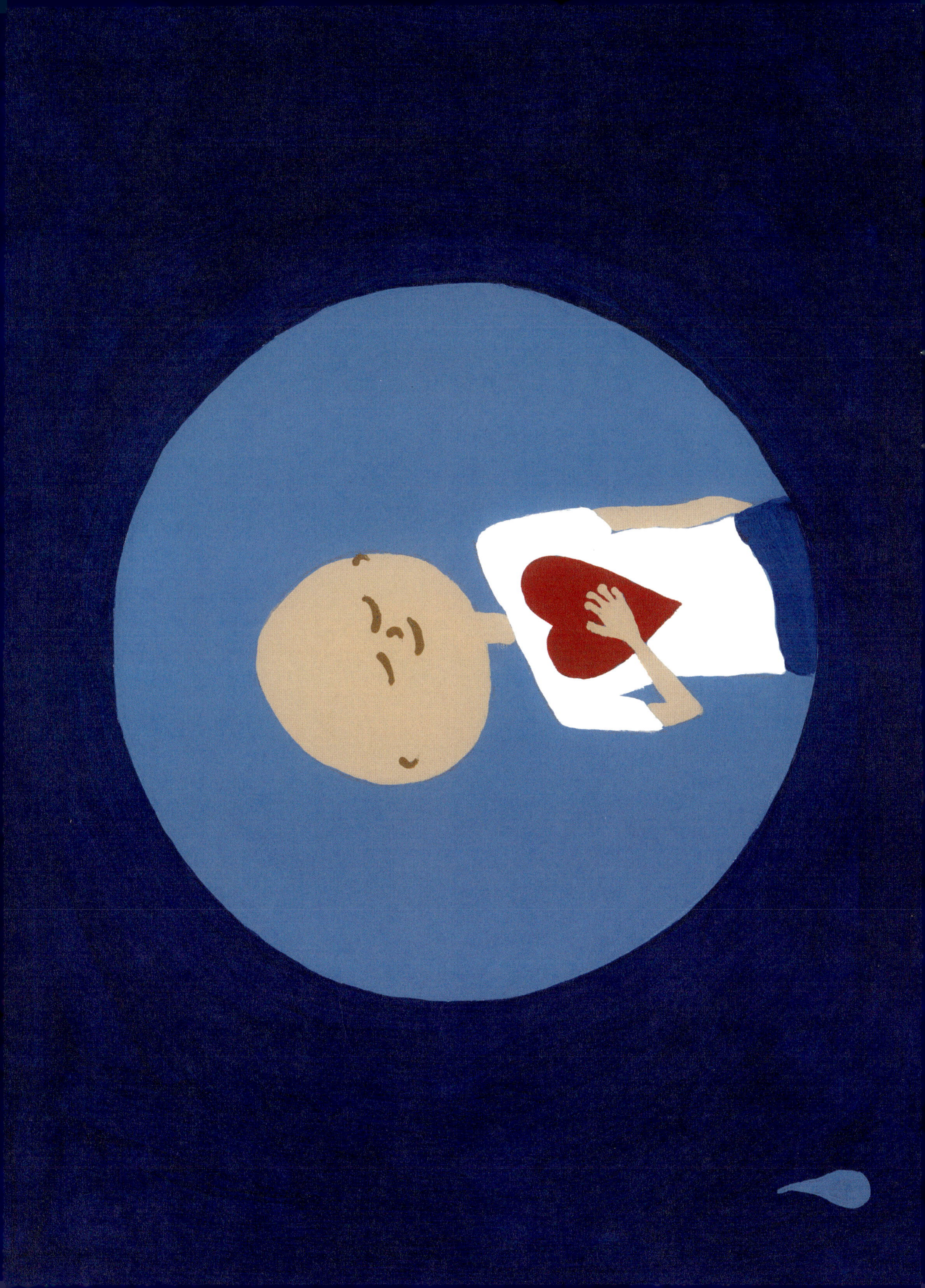

If I am being bullied
I could ask, "What's the best thing I can do?"
And listen quietly for a wise answer
That wisdom will send through.

Maybe it will say, "Tell my teacher."
But a louder voice says, "No, I shouldn't make a fuss."
Which one feels like the clear, knowing voice?
That's the wisdom we can trust!

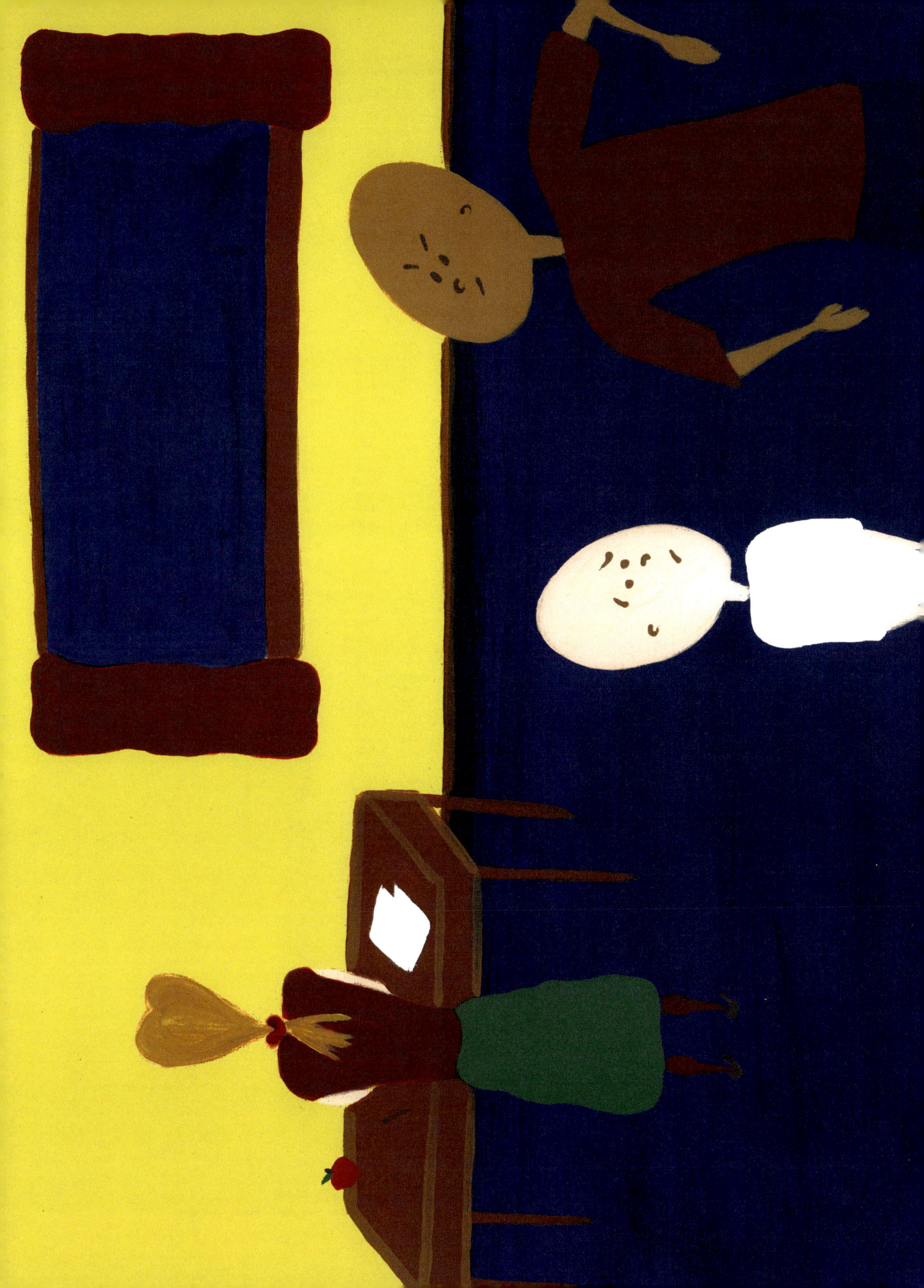

If I don't have an answer for a test
And I hear a voice say, "Cheat!"
Is that the voice of wisdom?
Is that who I really want to be?

Wisdom always tells us.
It's a feeling strong and calm,
And when we listen to it
We can't do any harm.

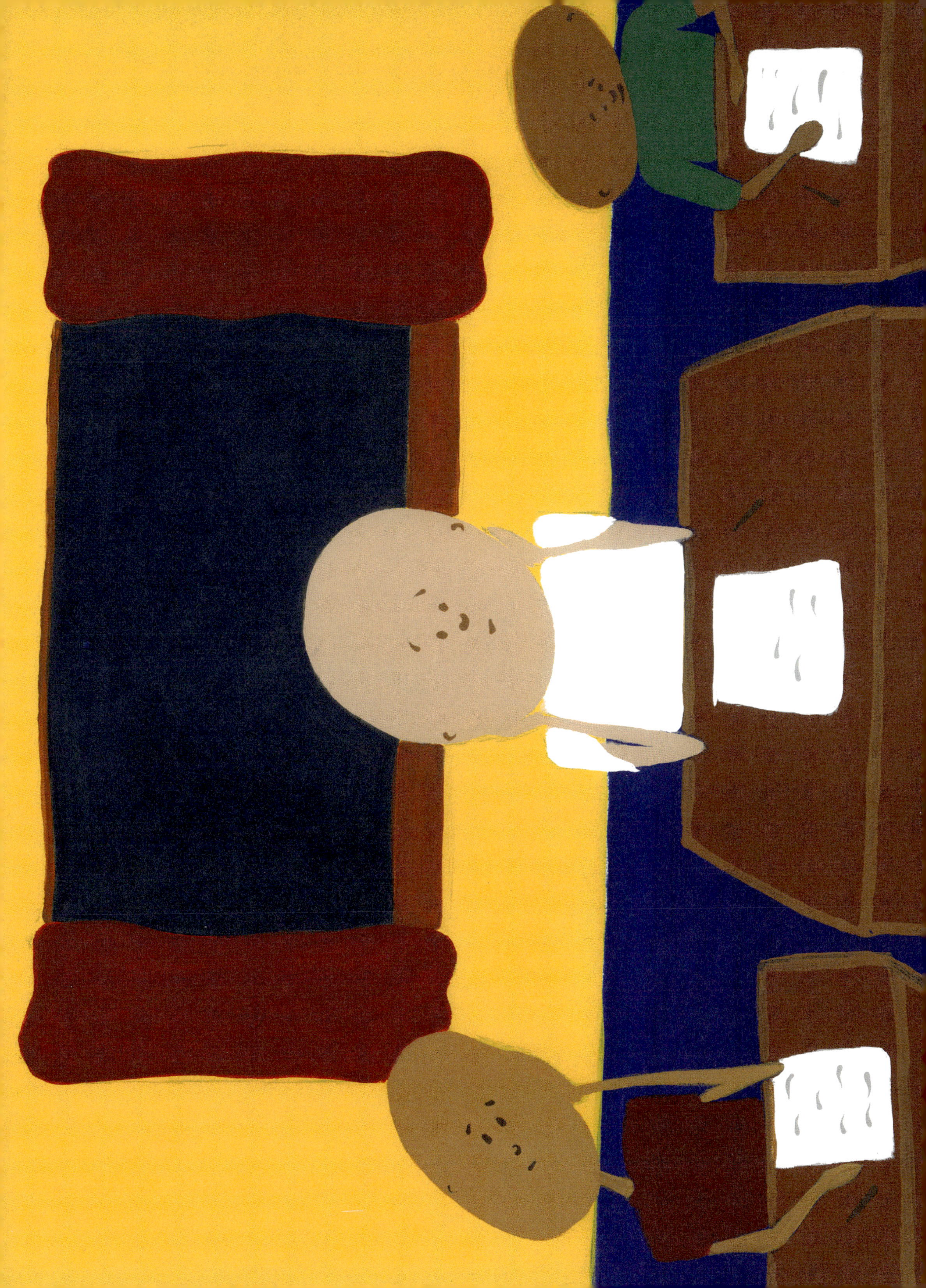

Sometimes even the strongest, smartest kids
And grown-ups, too, don't always act so wise,
Because their thoughts are tricking them.
They get all mixed up inside.

If they would only listen softly
They could truly hear
The wisdom inside singing
When their loud thinking clears.

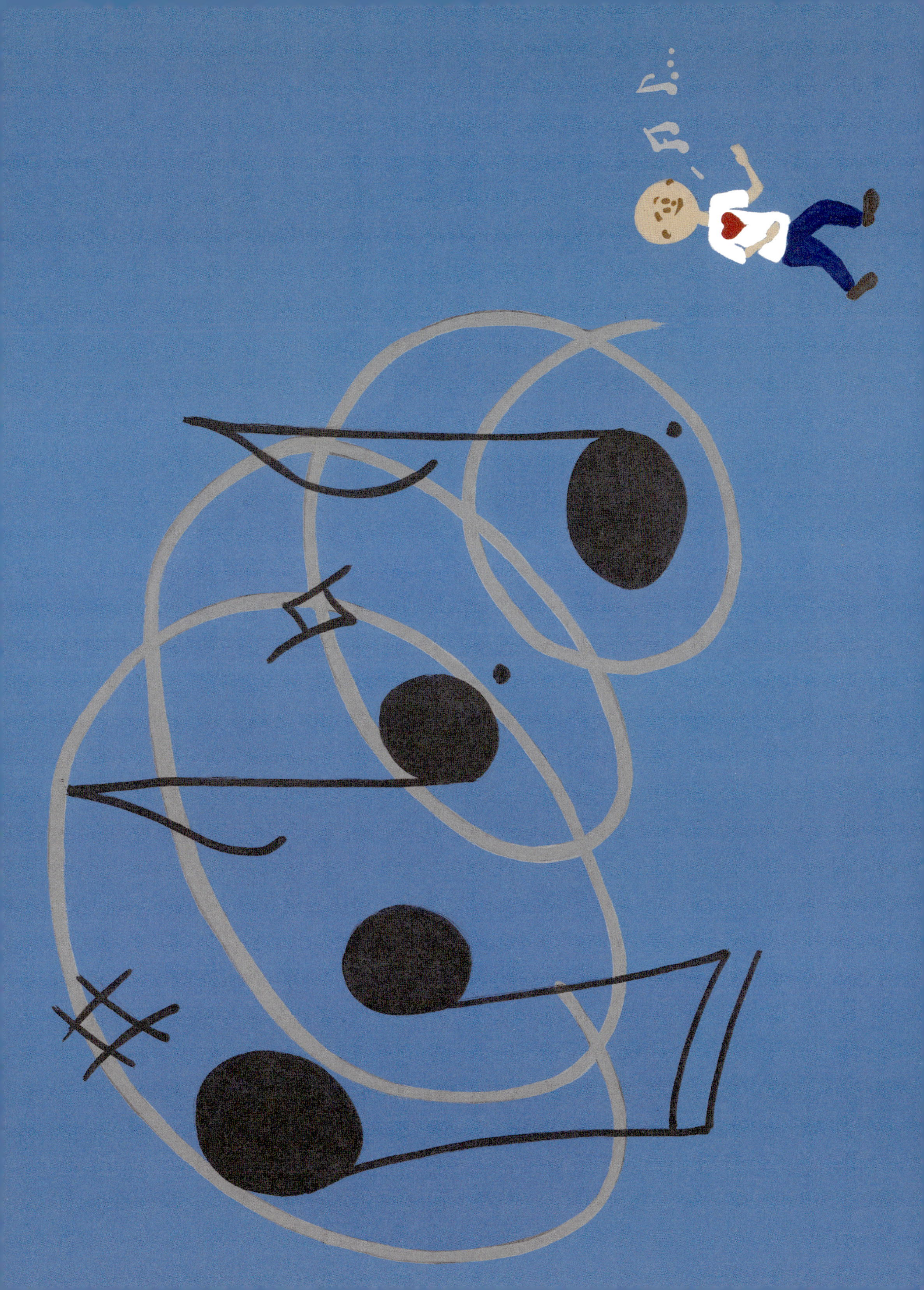

So what is wisdom?
Now I know!

Wisdom is a knowing.
Something just feels right.
From way deep inside,
We get an in-sight,
Like when a light bulb turns on at night
and fills the room with light.

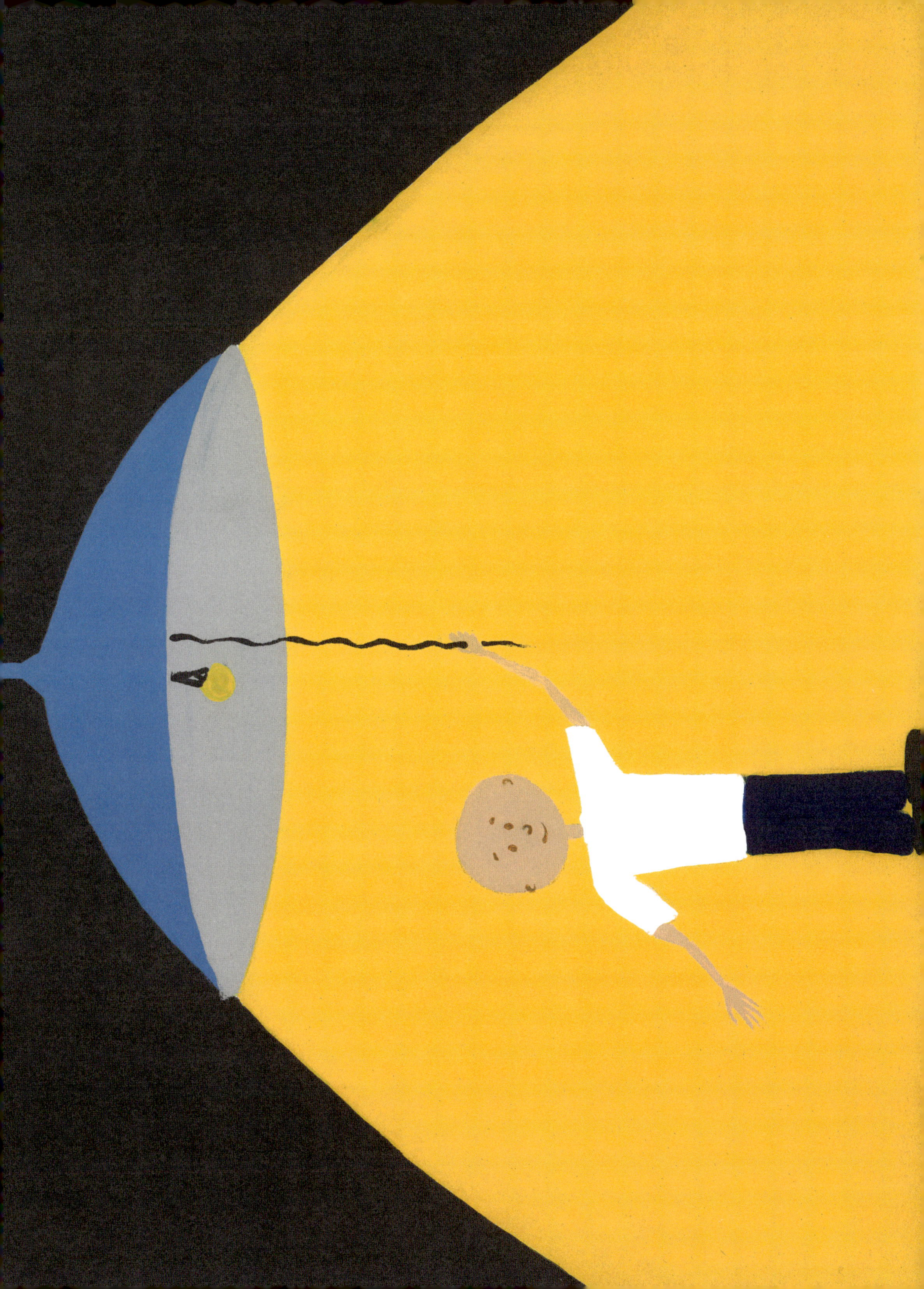

Like an unlimited fountain
That keeps bubbling up,
It's always there for us.
No matter what!

Wisdom is the way I see
The beauty that's inside of me,
And inside you and everyone else you know.
So let it shine and let it show,
And let it touch another's life
To pull them out of hurt and strife.
It's always there for us to touch
Like all the love we love so much.

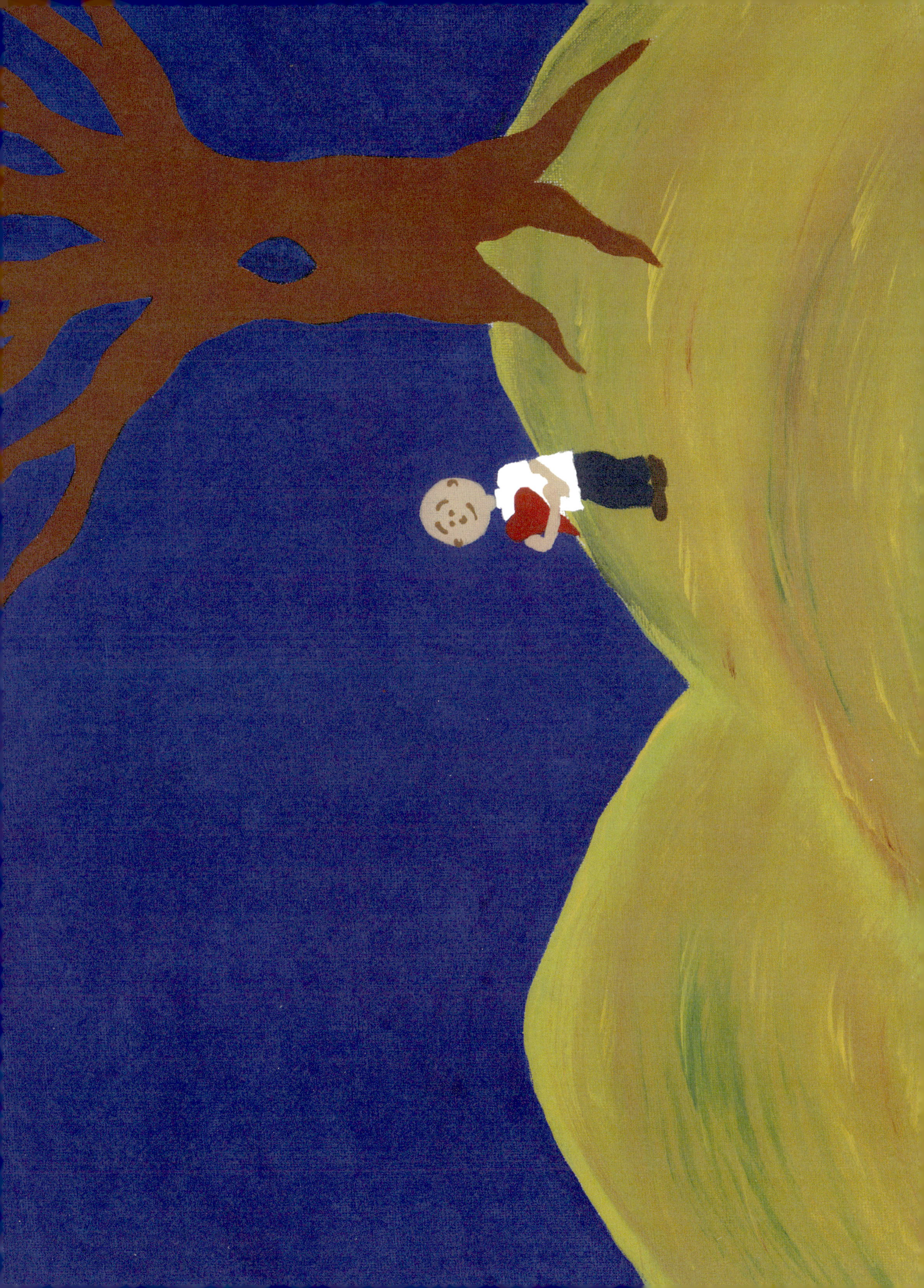

And the best news is...

I don't have to do anything to find it.
It'll find me when my mind gets quiet.

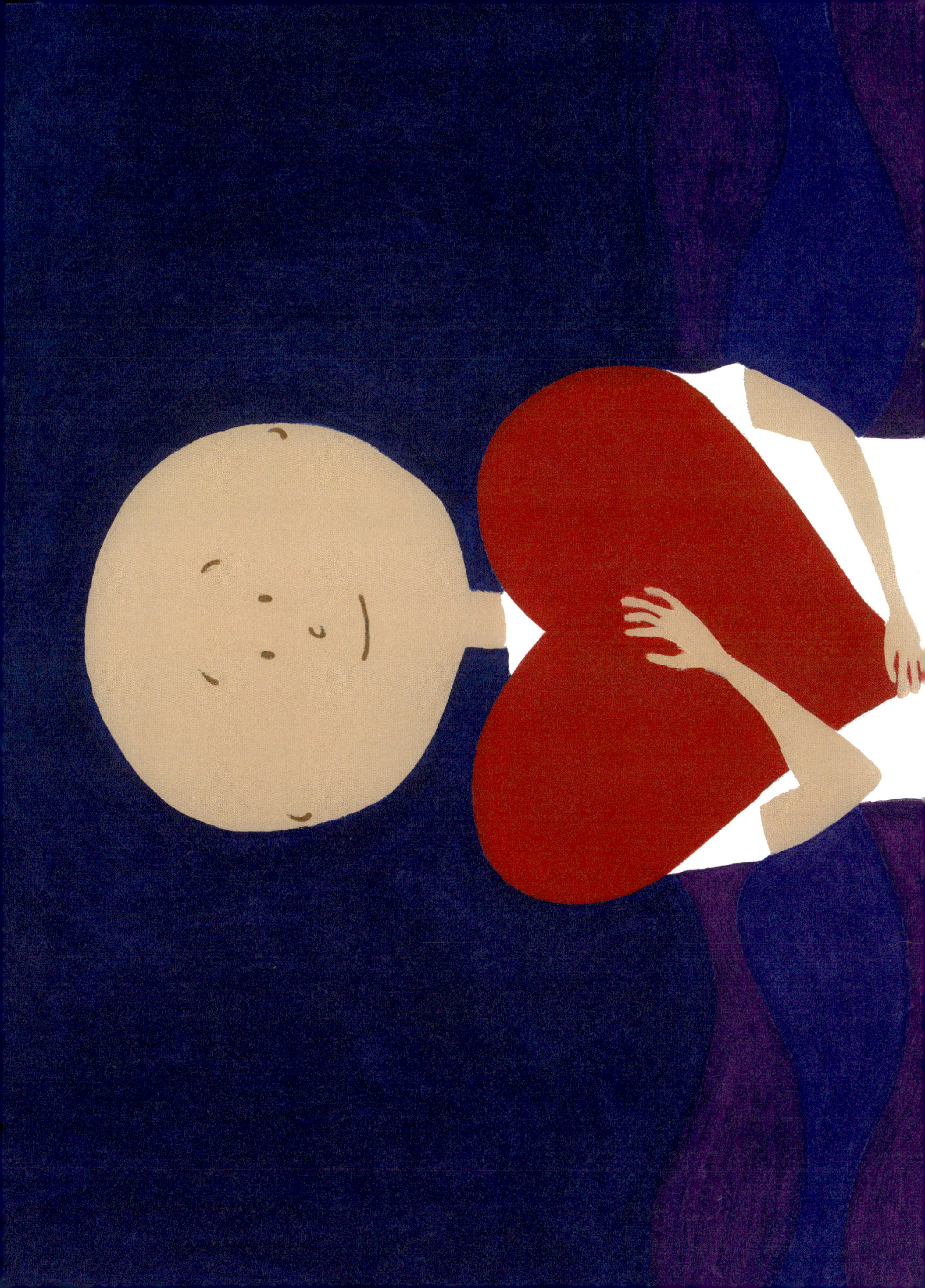

The End

(Or maybe a new beginning...)

Connecting Art to Real Life

Much of the art in this book purposely is abstract. As stated in What is a Thought?... "it teaches the storyline and whispers meaning but only to readers who can interpret it. Younger children as well as many students with social learning challenges may struggle to make these more abstract connections."

As such, to help young readers better understand the story and its relationship to the illustrations we have included an Art Glossary, with a short description of the meaning the artist and authors intended for each picture.

Additional questions are also provided at the end of the book to carry the discussion further and into deeper realms. All adults will benefit from reading through these sections. They offer questions that can be posed to readers of all ages to stimulate discussion on the notion of wisdom in a fun, engaging way.

As you read the story aloud consider encouraging children to guess what is going on in each picture. Explore different parts of the image and what each may convey; for instance, the setting, the heart, the music, the light, etc. Questions such as, "What emotion is the little guy feeling?" and "Do you think he is listening to his usual voice or to his voice of wisdom here?" will likely stimulate the child's involvement in the story. By doing so the children are encouraged to have thoughts of their own and experience for themselves how powerful wisdom can be when found.

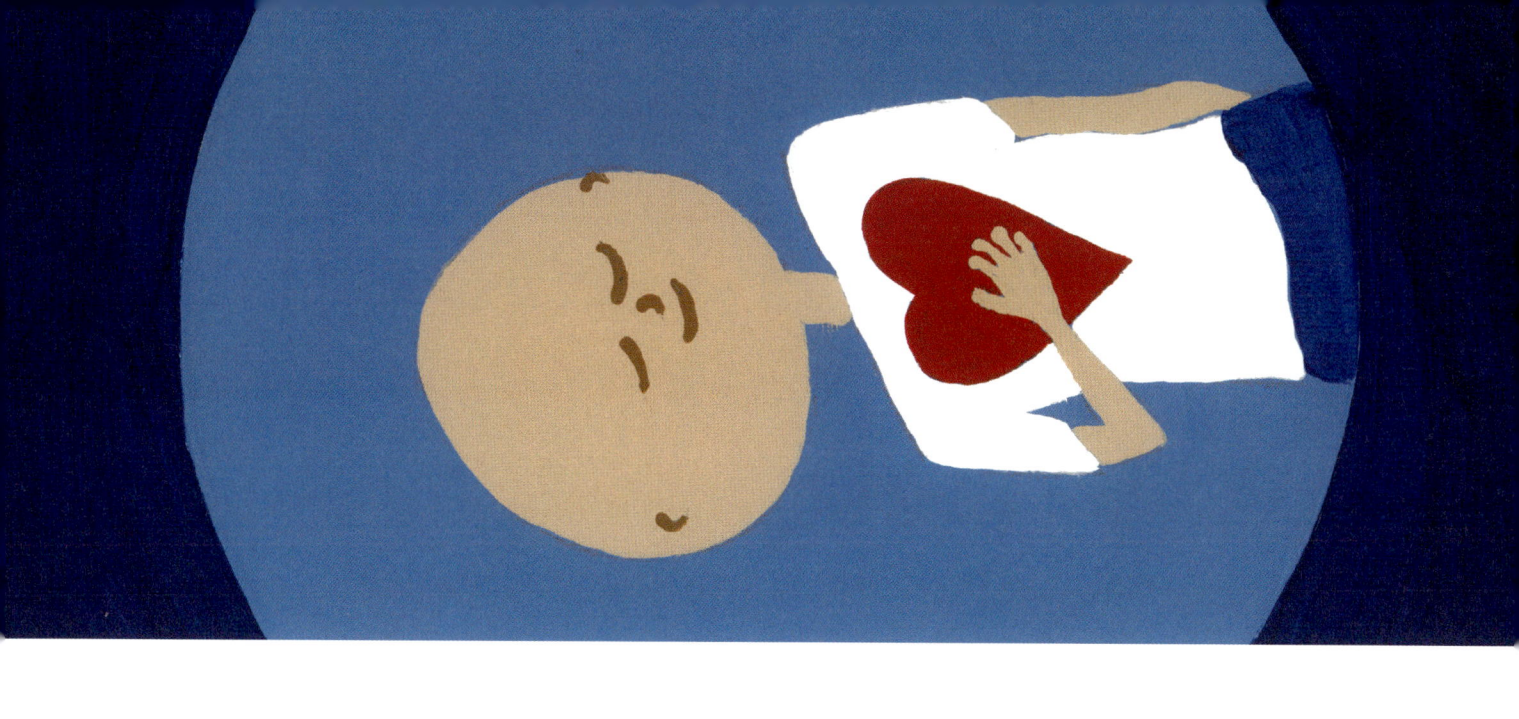

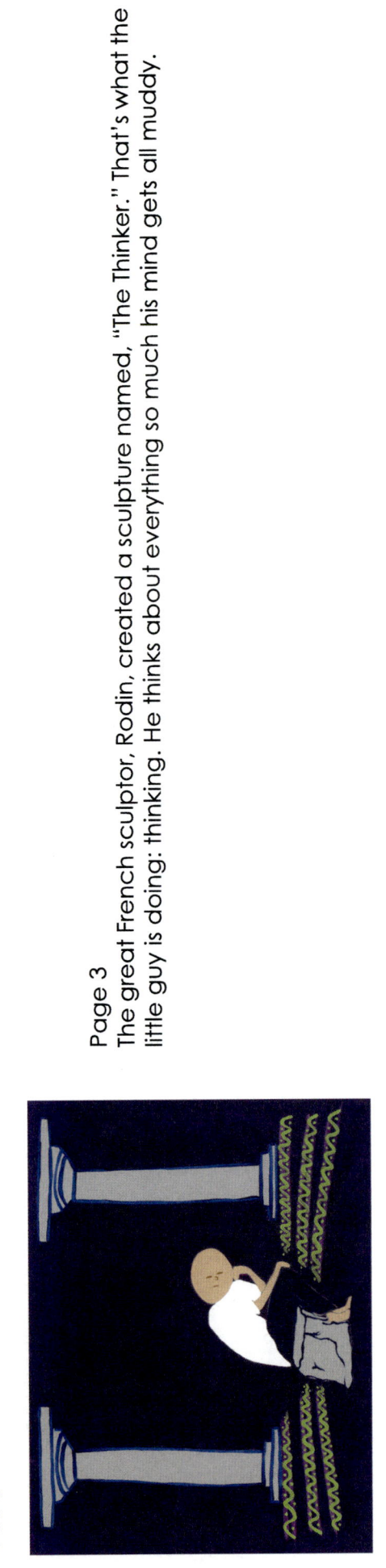

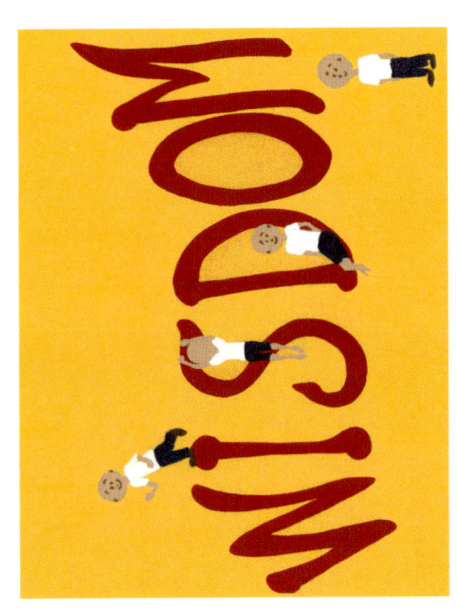

Page 3
The great French sculptor, Rodin, created a sculpture named, "The Thinker." That's what the little guy is doing: thinking. He thinks about everything so much his mind gets all muddy.

Page 5
"Wisdom" is such a BIG word. It sounds so smart. It sounds like mostly older people have it—not us. But maybe we could play with this word. What if we explored this big word more? If we did, maybe we would see something about wisdom that we never saw before.

Page 7
Little guy heard that wisdom is a good thing to have, and he wants some of it for himself, but he doesn't know where to find it. He looks everywhere in his house and can't find it.

Page 9
He looks everywhere outside, and he still can't find wisdom anywhere.

Page 11
Little guy heard about the wise old owl. He thinks maybe the owl knows where to find wisdom. So he goes off to find him, looks way up in the tree and asks him.

Page 13
Little guy gets so confused about what the owl said he feels like his head is going to explode. But all of a sudden he starts to see something new from inside.

Page 15
Old tortoise is supposed to be wise, too. Maybe he can help little guy figure out what wisdom is. So he knocks on his shell to wake him up.

Page 17
Out of little guy's complete confusion, all of a sudden he gets it. His head clears. He understands! It's like suddenly hearing trumpets or saxophones sound in his head: ta-dah!

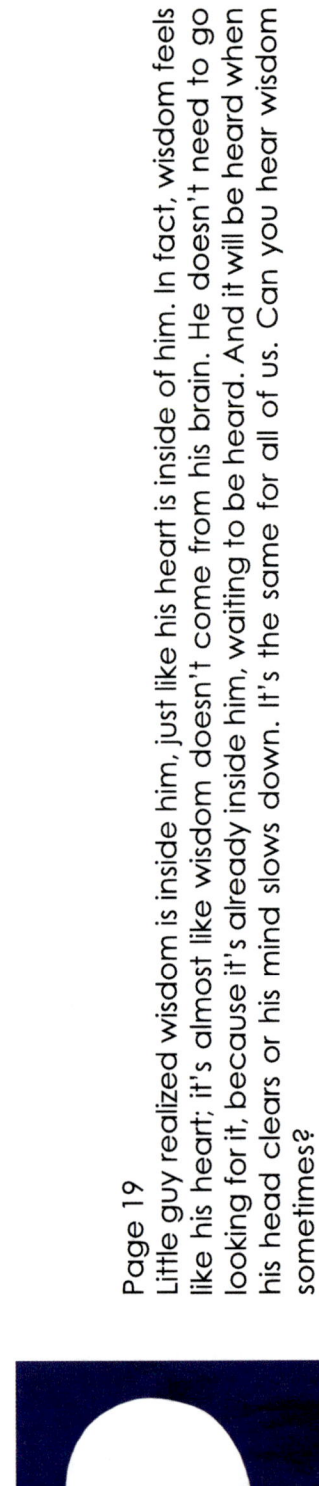

Page 19
Little guy realized wisdom is inside him, just like his heart is inside of him. In fact, wisdom feels like his heart; it's almost like wisdom doesn't come from his brain. He doesn't need to go looking for it, because it's already inside him, waiting to be heard. And it will be heard when his head clears or his mind slows down. It's the same for all of us. Can you hear wisdom sometimes?

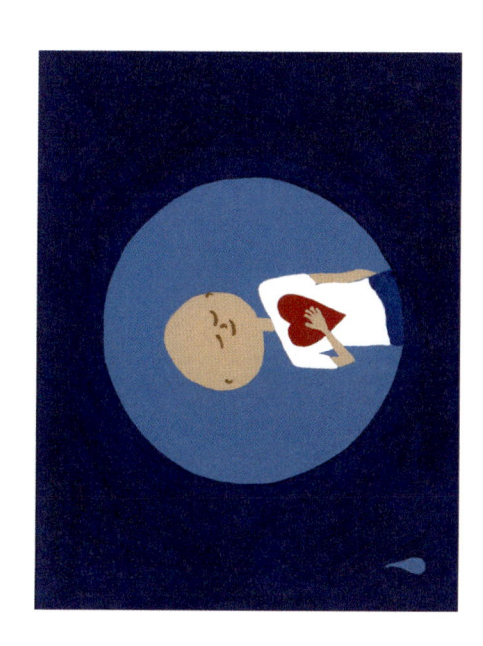

Page 21
Mmmm, it's such a yummy feeling to know wisdom is like love within us and can never go away, even when there are tears outside (or any other emotion).

Page 23
Okay, now that little guy knows where to find wisdom—from within—it's time to put it to the test in real life, like in his classroom with his teacher and other kids who might be bullies.

Page 25
Or, when little guy is taking a test and doesn't know the answer and is tempted to cheat, does he listen to the voice in his head that says "look at somebody else's answer," or does he listen to his inner voice of wisdom? He is the one who gets to decide which voice to listen to.

Page 27
He can tell the difference between the two voices because the inner voice of wisdom sounds like music to his ears, and he can always hear it inside when his mind calms down.

Page 29
Getting a flash of wisdom feels like a lightbulb turning on in his head.

Page 31
Little guy realizes he can take wisdom with him wherever he goes because it is inside of him. So can we! It's like a feeling in our gut, deep inside; we can feel it.

Page 33
Wisdom feels like love, because it is always there to guide us well through life. And all we have to do is listen quietly for it, because it never goes away.

Some suggested discussion questions

For teachers to use with their students or parents with their children during or after reading *What is Wisdom? (And Where do I find it?)*

A Note about Questions Provided

The listing of questions provided below is for the purpose of stimulating learning in the child or student. Each question is designed to be reflective and take the children into territory they may not be aware of. Some may think the questions too abstract or difficult for children of a young age. All we can say is, try them and you may be surprised at how much even young children are able to tap into their own wisdom and gain new perspective. And, if you don't like the questions provided, you may use your own.

These questions may be adjusted by the teacher or parent depending on the age, maturity level and learning capacity of the particular children/child. *It is highly recommended to first read the book all the way through, then go back through it and ask these questions.*

1. What do you suppose the little guy is doing [on page 1]? [*Thinking.*] What do you think he's thinking about?

2. He heard about a big word called "wisdom" and he's wondering what it is. What do you think wisdom is?

3. Do you know anyone who you think has wisdom? Who? What makes you think he or she is wise?

4. Where do you think that person found his or her wisdom?

5. What do you think wisdom would do for you if you had it?

6. Where do you think you could find wisdom?

7. Do you think the little guy would ever find wisdom in the places he's looking? Why or why not?

8. Have you heard of a "wise old owl?" Do you think the owl can give little guy the wisdom that it has? Why or why not?

9. What do you think the owl meant when he said to little guy, "I don't know how. I know. I just get a feeling. It's not in my head?"

10. Do you think little guy got confused about what the owl said? Once he got confused and couldn't figure out what the owl was talking about, what happened to little guy? [a new idea popped into his head]. Has a new idea ever popped into your head? Can anyone tell me what happened when it happened to you? Can you give me some examples?

11. Could that be what wisdom is? A new idea popping into our heads? Well, wisdom does come into us that way, but sometimes other thoughts that we've never had before also pop into our heads—sometimes angry or hurtful or hurting thoughts. Are those kinds of thoughts wisdom too?

12. How can we tell which new thoughts are wisdom and which aren't? What did the wise old owl say he gets? [A feeling] Could that mean our feelings can tell us whether it is wisdom or not? What kind of feeling might tell us it's thoughts of wisdom? [it's a feeling of knowing it's right. We feel it in our gut.]

13. After talking to the owl, where did little guy decide that wisdom comes from? [from inside ourselves; from our heart] What do you think that means?

14. But little guy got confused again and kept wondering. He said, if wisdom is inside him, why can't he always find it? Even if wisdom is always inside of you, can you always find it? Why? [Other louder thoughts block it out. It's still there; we just can't hear it.]

15. Little guy thought old tortoise would know why because an old tortoise is supposed to be wise, too; after all, he beat the bunny (hare) in a long race. But what do you think the tortoise meant when all he said was, "Slow down. That's the secret?"

16. Little guy had no idea what old tortoise meant, so he got confused again and frustrated. Then he figured he couldn't figure it out and he just gave up thinking about it anymore. Do you know why an answer popped into his head when he stopped trying so hard to think about it? [His head cleared. When our minds clear of all our other thinking, we can hear wisdom.]

17. What do you think little guy meant when he realized wisdom was behind all the noise? He could hear wisdom when his mind was doing what? [Doing nothing; quieting; relaxing; clearing; giving itself space for new thoughts from wisdom to come in]

18. Do you think it's true for you that your mind hears wisdom best when it is quiet or clear?

19. If your mind can only hear wisdom when it is quiet or clear, what is the opposite of a clear mind? What is your mind doing when it is pretty impossible to hear wisdom?

20. What do you think little guy meant when he said, "Wisdom is who I really am?" What does that mean to you?

21. If wisdom is really who we are inside, can it ever go away? [It can never go away. It's always there. We just can't hear it because our other thoughts get too noisy.]

22. Okay, so once again, if we want to hear wisdom, when do we have the best chance of hearing it? When our mind is doing what?

23. What does this mean to you: "I'll never be alone again, because I've got wisdom as my friend?"

24. Suppose we feel angry or hurt? Can we hear wisdom at those times?

25. Do you think wisdom can guide you about what to do when you run into a problem?

26. Like, what if you were being bullied by another kid. Well, first, is the bully listening to his or her wisdom? Why or why not?

27. Okay, so if you were being bullied, would you want to listen to wisdom to help you know how to best deal with it? How could you have the best chance of hearing wisdom in this situation?

28. How can you tell the difference between the voice of wisdom telling you what to do, and some other kind of voice telling you what to do?

29. If you didn't know the answers on a test, and you heard a voice in your head telling you that you should cheat, is that the voice of wisdom? How do you know?

30. What kind of feeling comes along with wisdom? [strong and calm—you just know it is right. You have no question that it might be wrong. You just feel it!]

31. If you had the thought that you wanted to steal candy from a store or a necklace that you liked but didn't have enough money for, do you think that would be the voice of wisdom? How would you know?

32. Can you think of any other examples where a problem might come up and you could decide whether to listen to wisdom or not?

33. Do you think wisdom has to do with how old you are? Why or why not? Have you ever seen or heard of any older people who have not acted very wise? Have you ever heard of or seen any younger kids act wise? So does age have anything to do with it?

34. All that's needed to hear wisdom is for our thinking to do what? [stop, or calm down or quiet or clear]

35. What makes wisdom like a light bulb turning on in the dark?

36. What do you think it means when the story says, wisdom "is always there for us to touch"?

37. And what do you think it means when it says, "And the best news is… I don't have to do anything to find it. It'll find me when my mind gets quiet."?

38. What do you think all this means for you and your life at school and at home?

39. What do you think all this means for you and your life with your friends?

A Note about Where to Find Lesson Plans and Activities, If Interested

What is a Thought? (A Thoughts Is a Lot) by Jack Pransky and Amy Kahofer, published by Think Social Publishing*, offers lessons and learning activities on an included CD intended to enhance learning of *What is a Thought?*...

Some of these lesson plans and learning activities pertain directly to this book, *What is Wisdom (and Where Do I Find It)?*, specifically...

Lesson 4. Calm Mind Thinking vs. Upset Mind Thinking.
  Activity: The Glitter Jar
  Activity: Exploring Calm vs. Mixed-up Thought.

Lesson 10. Sun and Clouds (with handout).

Note to adults reading this book to children:

The most important life lessons for all the children you read this book to are:

❖ Every child (and adult) has wisdom within.
❖ This wisdom can be heard when the mind clears of its usual thinking.
❖ Wisdom is heard through new insight.
❖ Every child has the ability to realize his/her own insights.
❖ Every child has the ability to recognize clues that someone else has had an insight.

As you read this book look for opportunities to get little ones to pay attention to insights.

After reading the book, ask each child to be still and remember when a special, big idea just popped into his or her head. For example, refer back to the light bulb picture on page 29. See what comes out. Just let the conversation flow. [Note: If it feels right in any moment, this could even be done by stopping while reading the book.]

Ask the children where they think insights come from. Let the conversation flow.
Ask the children if they ever saw someone else have an insight. Again let the conversation flow. The point is to hear what the children already know and what they have experienced about insights.
Trust that you can explore what they think an insight did for them or for someone else.
Let yourself learn from the children; they may surprise you. Along the way see if you, yourself can learn answers to the following questions: Did they realize something new? Did their insights help someone else? What was their feeling like when they had the insight? How did they know someone else had had an insight? What did the children notice other people do or say? Let the children teach you.

[Note: Thank you to Kathy Marshall for her assistance with this section.]

Other books by Jack Pransky and Amy Kahofer

Pransky, J., & Kahofer, A. (2013). *What is a thought? (A thought is a lot)*. San Jose, CA: Social Thinking Publishing. [A children's picture book]

Other books by Jack Pransky

Pransky, J. (2011). *Somebody Should Have Told Us!* British Columbia, Canada: CCB Publishing.

Pransky, J. (2011). *Modello: A story of hope for the inner-city and beyond*. British Columbia, Canada: CCB Publishing

Pransky, J. (2012). *Parenting from the Heart*. British Columbia, Canada: CCB Publishing

Pransky, J. (2003). *Prevention from the Inside-Out*. Bloomington, IN: AuthorHouse

Pransky, J. (2015). *Paradigm Shift*. British Columbia, Canada: CCB Publishing

Pransky, J. and Carpenos, L. (2000). *Healthy Thinking/Feeling/Doing from the Inside-Out: A middle school curriculum and guide for the prevention of violence, abuse and other problem behaviors*. Brandon, VT: Safer Society Press.

Made in the USA
Middletown, DE
09 February 2020